STRUGGLING HEARTIST

JOSH LAWSON

Bambaz Press

Los Angeles, 2019

Book design: Baz Here
Cover art: Baz Here
Editor: Bambi Here

ISBN: 9781097462995
Printed in the United States of America

Bambaz Press
548 S Spring Street
Suite 1201
Los Angeles, California 9013 USA

bambi@bambazpress.com

Author's note –

It's been said that America and Australia are two countries separated by a common language. Such is certainly the case with my poetry. As a native Australian, I write with the Australian accent in my head, which dictates my rhyme. This means I will sometimes write a perfect rhyme in the Australian accent but an imperfect rhyme to the American ear. For instance – *more* and *jaw* are perfect rhymes when spoken in Australian, but the American tongue makes the two words imperfect partners.

To my American friends, if it's any consolation, I've opted for your spelling. For example, words like *flavour* and *apologise* will become *flavor* and *apologize*. So, while you are somewhat shortchanged when this poetry is spoken, I hope I slightly repay the debt when it is read.

And lastly, thank you to both countries for inspiring me in different ways, and for both being so full of clever, creative and kind people, many of whom played crucial roles in making this book possible.

Josh

This book is dedicated to the incredible women I've given my heart to, who allowed me to love so much that it turned into poetry.

CONTENTS

TWO STONES

In a field, by a hill,
Lay two stones, very still—
One was round, one was flat like a sandwich.
And indeed, if you'd seen them,
The distance between them
Wasn't much more than half of one hand-width.

They had been there together
For what felt like forever,
Though they'd ne'er spoken once to each other.
You see, both stones construed
This great hush as just rude
And they each blamed the silence on t'other.

Until one dusty morning,
The wind blew without warning
And the flat stone stirred ever so slightly.
It then sneezed once or twice,
And so just to be nice,
The round stone said, "Bless you," politely.

Now these words were a shock—
Heretofore, either rock
Had not talked to the one that had flanked it.
So when the flat stone decided
To swallow its pride, it
Looked straight to the round stone and thanked it.

"You're welcome," replied
The round stone as it tried
To sound natural and pleasant about it.
The flat stone said, "Surely,
I do hope I'm not poorly."
And the round stone responded, "I doubt it."

And the flat one came back
With a pithy comeback
And they laughed at the stone's exclamation.
Then the next thing they knew,

Thanks to one stone's "bless you,"
They were lost in a rich conversation.

In a talkative haze
The hours became days
And they bantered without flap or fuss.
In exuberant tones
It occurred to the stones
There was much that the pair could discuss.

And as things often go
In the strange to and fro
Of life's unpredictable fashion,
What started as neighborly
Grew more and more favorably
Until it exploded with passion.

The round stone then stated,
"I'm a fool to have waited
So long before speaking, my treasure."
"Why, it's simply absurd,"
The flat stone concurred,
"That a sneeze finally brought us together."

And when the round stone was sure
It could stand it no more
It cried, "Kiss me! Oh, kiss me this minute!"
But the flat stone did not;
It stayed right in its spot
And it wept till no tears were left in it.

The round stone asked, "Why,
My love, do you cry?
Is it something I've done to upset you?"
And the flat stone said, "No.
You've done nothing but show
Me how great love can be since I met you."

"The reason I stall
Is I've no legs to crawl,
And no arms to reach you, it's true.
So, the inches that break us

Feel like thousands of acres
For I cannot come closer to you."

While they felt they could hold a
Love big as a boulder,
They were each of them only a stone.
Though the gap wasn't much,
It was too great to touch,
And they both could not feel more alone.

Then in fear and dismay
They knew not what to say
And a hush sprang up much like before.
It turned into a quiet
And though neither knew why, it
Turned into a silence once more.

And the stones sit there still,
In a field, by a hill,
Where naught can be heard but the breeze.
One stone is flat,
One is round next to that,
And they both pray the other will sneeze.

MOUTHS

It all began that fateful night my eyes befell your lovely face—
A beauty blistered in my brain that no nepenthe could replace,
For as I drifted down and deep into the dark of sleep's embrace,
Fine fantasies and flights of you fandangoed round my mind apace.

I woke to find the palm of my right hand tormented by an itch.
Investigating further it appeared to be a hollow which
Presented like an inch-long scar that someone, somehow did unstitch.
A bloodless wound that oped and closed with every alternating twitch.

The edges of the little hole—a perfect, puffy, pinky band
Beyond which lay what looked to be a set of tongue and tonsils, and
Two rows of teeny teeth which made me finally now understand
It was a mouth, a tiny mouth that lay inside my open hand.

A sudden rush of horror and alarm cascaded over me.
It seemed so blatantly unfair, so cruel, so mean, so arbit'ry
That I should be the victim of this medical anomaly—
A second mouth appearing in a place where mouths just should not be.

I supposed that if I hid my hand, this ugliness I could ignore,
Were't not for the distressing presentation of a couple more.
Two extra Lilliputian mouths upon my wrist, then three, then four,
Emerging up my arm and neck—so many I could not keep score.

The multitude of mini mouths began to grow and grow and grow,
Popping up all over me for reasons that I didn't know,
So fast that by the time I took my clothes off I discovered, lo
A hundred thousand little mouths adorned my body head to toe.

Up and down my legs and arms, across my back and chest and hips,
My face, my feet, my ears, my knees, my shoulder blades, my fingertips.
And consternation soon gave way to panic as I came to grips
With disappearing underneath these countless pairs of open lips.

As strange as this dark torment was, it was to get much stranger still
For suddenly I felt a hunger so completely stark and shrill;
A hunger that consumed me whole, a hunger blossoming until
It felt as though my mouths had stomachs each that they required I fill.

I started feeding all my mouths with anything that I could find—

From chocolate chips, to frozen peas, to stale bread, to bacon rind.
But nothing satisfied the hundred thousand little mouths maligned,
Still crippled was I by their hundred thousand little needs combined.

And while I slumped in desperation in a heap upon the floor,
I heard a feeble voice beside my ear that whispered softly, "More."
Then looking in the mirror to a little mouth upon my jaw
I noticed that it drew a breath and once again it cried out "More."

Then too, a mouth below my neck pled "More," and then without delay
Another mouth was speaking, then a dozen more had joined the fray.
It didn't take too long before they all had cottoned on and they
Were crying out like hungry babes, and "More" was all the mouths could say.

This solitary word appeared to be their only stock and store,
The greedy repetitious mantra calling to me o'er and o'er.
And louder did each holler get with ev'ry deafening encore—
In booming iterations, it was clear that they all wanted more.

But empty was my house of any foodstuff that the mouths could chew.
I could not leave for certainly my freakishness was in plain view.
Then clarity descended and it dawned on me what I should do,
And reaching for the phone with mouthy fingers I did call for you.

You came the very instant that you heard my melancholy plea.
Though I had anxious doubts with which I wrestled momentarily—
These teeming, testy, tiny mouths I did not want your eyes to see.
But in the end, I had no choice—their hunger was too great for me.

I opened up the door for you while in my chest my poor heart raced.
I stood there in my complicated nakedness and dumbly braced
To be insulted, scorned or mocked, to be heartbroken and disgraced.
Instead, you threw your arms around me fervently and we embraced.

The second that my mouths were pressed against your perfect, porcelain skin
They cried for more no more, and silently they gorged and drank you in.
Their hunger being quashed by touch, like agony by heroin.
The proof of satisfaction in each separate, selfish, greedy grin.

Yes, every mouth was settled as you pulled your body into mine.
You cloyed the lips upon my back when your bare stomach found my spine.
I surfeited on you as if your body was expensive wine,
Consuming every single part, for every part I found divine.

A peculiar thing then happened, as this weary poet reminisces—
Once the aggregation of these former bottomless abysses
Supped on your exquisiteness, the now contented orifices
Disappeared forever with a hundred thousand goodbye kisses.

And vanish though they did, they left behind for me a hopeless fate:
A constant craving sharp and hard, a lusty longing vast and great.
I have in me a hunger still no food or drink or place can sate.
My hunger is a burning one, that only *you* can satiate.

And though they've not returned, the multiplicity of mouths galore,
One mouth remains, the mouth you kiss, the mouth I started with before.
And while I have you close to me, my darling, you can now be sure
My single, solitary mouth will always, always ask for more.

COLLISION

His life

Moving fast

In one direction

Looking nowhere but forward

Her life

Just as fast

Approaching from the left

Seeing nothing but what is straight ahead

Two lives

Gaining momentum

Their speed the same

Their destinations different

Both blinded by ambition

Deafened by distraction

Muted by fatigue

And then

Perhaps inevitably

They collide

With calamitous force

And devastating discord

The smash takes its toll

First the flesh

Burning hot

Melting together

Unable to be pulled apart

Then their plans, their best-laid plans

Exploding into ash

Irreparable

Irretrievable

Irreversible

Then their hearts

Liquefying

Bubbling

Smoldering under the intensity

Only when they cool will they harden again

But then they will be unrecognizable

And memories, so many memories

Stories

Souvenirs from collisions past

Sent flying

Lodging in the other

Making space where there was no space

Finding room

But the lives come each with time

And the impact claims that too

Taking from one

Giving to the other

So that time is not stolen

It is never stolen

It is replaced

And the wreckage

Though cataclysmic

Is not fatal

So, the lives roll on

Stronger for the shock

Moving even faster now

In the same direction

Unburdened by plans

Unaware of fatigue

Undone by her

Undone by him

No, the collision was not fatal

Though two lives were lost

Yes

Two lives were lost

FALLING

I'm sinking like zinc through the cold and thin air
Hands failing to find finger holds that aren't there
Then panic's replaced by denial, then prayer
But the fall crushes all to make room for despair

Gravity grips with a vexed animosity
Far beyond terminal this cruel velocity
Fear chokes my heart with such fervent ferocity
That dreams of the end plague my dark curiosity

Closed are my eyes, turning all black from blue
Dynamics dictating that soon I'll be through
But destiny knows more than science and I do
For below me, awaiting my impact, is you

Toward a swift death my body careens
But death doesn't come as fate intervenes
And before the blow splits me into smithereens
Your arms bear the bombshell like two trampolines

My speed slows to nothing as I come to rest
In the softness and safeness of your welcome breast
Inertia dissolves at physics request
And I find terra firma in the warmth of your chest

Then off like a shot we soar into the sky
Gravity can't catch us now as we fly
Through earth's atmosphere, we're weightless and I
Am no longer scared now that you are nearby

We swim round the sun with a fire in our face
And dance on the moon while the tides shift their place
We kiss on the stars while the comets give chase
Naked together, falling upwards in space

THE GREY WOLF

Deep within the forest's hush,
Past brake and bramble, briar and brush,
There lived a wolf of main and might
Whose pelt was blacker than the night.
A lone wolf was he for, alack,
He'd never had his own wolf pack.
Though truthfully, within his heart,
The lonely years had made him start
To feel the stiff and steady sting
Of sorrow, so each night he'd bring
His face up to the moonlit sky
And send to it his doleful cry.
Then one night in the woods nearby,
He heard a female wolf reply.
And when her hungry howl came back
He finally knew he'd have his pack.
For there within the wicked wild
The sable wolf conceived a child.
And soon thereafter he'd another,
Giving his first born a brother.
Then a third. Then number four.
Then a fifth. And then no more.
No girl among them, no not one.
Without exception, each his son.
The black wolf knew that every whelp
Would need his wisdom and his help
To bear the heartless hinterland.
And so, he diligently planned
To teach each boy one skill and then
He'd send them to the woods as men.
The skill he thought the first would need
Would be the fortitude to lead.
He taught that cub to guard the pack,
To keep it safe, to watch its back,
And when the world would do its worst
The boy would put his family first.
Although it took a heavy toll,
The eldest cub took on the role.
And with the steadfast strength of cedar,

The first born son became a leader.
The black wolf then in likewise fashion,
Taught his second born compassion.
He gifted him the crucial art
Of acting not of head, but heart.
And loyalty, the young one learned,
Would mean his care would be returned.
And though his instincts were to kill,
He'd choose instead to show good will.
And with that lesson now imparted,
The second born became kind-hearted.
To the third of his descendants,
The black wolf taught him independence.
The eager, little cub was shown
To solve life's problems on his own.
And if abstracted from the clade
He'd never need another's aid,
For harder is't to prick the skin
When one is armored from within.
And as the pup was so compliant,
The third born wolf grew self-reliant.
Then to the next he did reveal
The fourth in line would master zeal.
With stern instruction, he made sure
His son would always strive for more.
For dreams were vain, the black wolf knew,
Unless you made those dreams come true.
And if he failed, he'd now possess
An ache that ever-craved success.
And though that ache would feel malicious,
The fourth born wolf became ambitious.
Then lastly, the black wolf declaimed
Unto his youngest—be untamed.
For happy would the young pup be
If he could set his spirit free.
And in a world of wolves and sheep
This wolf would follow not a keep.
When footprints marked the trail ahead,
He'd choose the trackless path instead.
And frightening though it was to start
Became, the fifth born, wild at heart.

Satisfied he'd taught each quin,
The black wolf then did leave his kin.
For though he'd longed to have this pack,
He now longed for his loneness back.
His boys, he thought, would be alright,
And so he disappeared from sight.
And many seasons from that day—
How many it was hard to say—
The wolf returned, this time to stay,
His once black coat, now charcoal grey.
That lonely sting had brought him back
To find again his kindred pack.
He knew his lone wolf days were done
When first he saw his eldest son
A cub no more, but fully grown,
And now with family of his own.
His son forgot not the advice
That leadership meant sacrifice.
His family first, that was the gem,
So all he had he gave to them.
Which meant that when the grey wolf tried
To stay a while he was denied.
His son had not the time to spare
So they moved on and left him there.
The grey wolf had no time to mourn
Before he found his second born.
But once again, the wolf of grey
Was e'er so gently turned away.
You see, the swollen-hearted brother
Loved with all that heart another.
That was how he'd learned to live
And now he'd no more love to give.
So off he went, filled with desire
To find his wolf and leave his sire.
When he found his third born son
Prowling in a pack of one,
The grey wolf thought that surely he'd
Have something that this boy would need.
Alas, his son was most proficient,
Being always self sufficient.
And though his father had returned,

That did not change the lesson learned.
For he, thanks to his keen resilience,
Lived a life of breadth and brilliance.
He'd never needed help before
So he forsook his once mentor.
The grey wolf searched the forest floor
Until he found son number four.
The wolf was sprinting through the trees—
His parent trailed with great unease—
He would not, could not, ever halt.
Perhaps it was his father's fault
For teaching him as he was bred
That there'd always be more ahead.
So charmed by want and fueled by need
The driven wolf picked up his speed.
But speed comes not along with grey,
Therefore his son did race away.
His fifth born boy, he could not find,
Although a trail was left behind.
His tread was tracked where'er it went
But naught was found, except a scent.
The problem with a maverick pup
Is that it's tricky to keep up.
Thus, all he'd left of flesh and blood
Were just some paw prints in the mud.
The truth, he now could sadly tell
Was that he'd taught his sons too well.
And when would fade the afternoon
He'd howl unto the crescent moon,
Though not so that the land would fear him
But rather so his boys could hear him.
And they did listen every night
Until his grey coat turned to white.
No matter where the pack would stray,
The white wolf's voice would find its way.
The wolves felt comfort in his cry
For now they knew he was nearby.
But as the years did steal his might,
His bays fell softer in the night.
And slowly would his cries decrease
'Til altogether they did cease.

The night sky then did come alive
With not the voice of one, but five.
Moaning all for one more chance
To hear upon the night's expanse
Their father's voice, for they were rent,
They knew just what his silence meant.
The wolf once black, then grey, then white
Now watches over them each night.
And though he cannot holler back,
He hears the voices of his pack.
For while his wolfish boys still prowl
They howl
  And howl
    And howl
      And howl

THE MAN MADE OUT OF CLAY

I've a story to tell that might leave in its wake
The pang of distress and dismay,
And whether it ends with hope or heartache
I'd rather not yet say.
Just let me unveil the sorrowful tale
Of the man made out of clay.

A regular man, I suppose you could say,
Like anyone else you might know,
Except the poor fellow was made out of clay
Complete from top to toe.
T'was not hard to spot a man of terra cotta and
So, his shame did grow.

He'd look in the mirror to stare at his shape
And he hated all he saw—
A cage made of clay that he longed to escape,
Alone to his loamy core.
He knew in his blood, that was made out of mud,
He could stand this pain no more.

He pressed at his cheeks and he pulled at his chin
And the clay shifted under his touch.
He reshaped his face when he pushed on his skin,
He poked and he prodded and such.
He thought looking thin might help him within
But sadly, it did not help much.

So, he took to his body, his arms and his chest
And he squeezed between fingers and thumb.
And then, like a sculptor, he took to the rest—
His shoulders, his legs and his bum.
He thought looking bigger might possibly trigger
Relief, but alas there was none.

He meddled and modeled and molded but still
The rust-brown man was blue.
He almost gave up on the whole thing until
He realized what he had to do—

To change things indeed, he decided that he'd
Remove a piece or two.

He'd only start small, almost nothing at all,
Just a bit from here and there.
And after he scooped away each little ball
He'd throw it aside without care
But it wasn't enough, he abhorred too much stuff
And he felt he had more clay to spare.

So the pieces got larger; he hacked at his flesh,
Tearing hunks and handfuls away.
A fervor took over, and in his blind thresh
He forgot what had once caused dismay.
The more he'd remove, the more it did prove
The problem was not in the clay.

Though the pieces grew bigger, the man: he did not,
As the chunks piled up on the floor.
Smaller and smaller and smaller he got,
Until he could take nothing more.
But the ache did remain, that terrible pain,
No peace in those pieces for sure.

The man made of clay, no longer a man
But rather the sum of each part.
In hundreds of segments he searched for a plan,
When it hit him where he had to start.
For there he could see, among the debris,
In halves, his broken heart.

All that was left was to rebuild from scratch,
He would gather his pieces and then—
If his hands, now detached, could build halves that would match
He might be a whole person again.
But the two different hands had two different plans,
And instead they built two different men.

Smaller than he from whom both men had burst,
They looked like identical kin.
Each one believing that he'd been the first,
So each one was shocked by his twin—

The same head, the same face, they took up the same space,
A double from outside to in.

The two men of clay stood and stared at each other
And they both rather liked what they saw.
They viewed not with hate, but with love for their brother
And neither could find any flaw.
Each saw his worth clearer, not by spying a mirror
But by eyeing himself a bit more.

They hugged one another in a caring embrace,
Their clay bits combined now as one,
When right through the window they happened to face
Came streaming the hot midday sun.
Like a kiln, it then charred their soft bodies hard,
Their changing days evermore done.

Herein ends the tale, with nature's cruel trick,
The sculpture fore'er on display.
Perhaps you can see now that he's turned to brick
The tale's not so sad, in a way.
He's back to one piece now, and finally found peace now—
The man made out of clay.

CAKE

Serves two

Preparation time: life until this moment

Cooking time: life after this moment

INGREDIENTS

2 people (gender not important)
1 teaspoon attraction
1 handful bravado
2 1/2 cups insecurities
2 heaped spoonfuls intimacy
3 tablepoons secrets
4 eggs
1 cup expectations
5-6 sprigs of time
2 1/2 cups familiarity
2 hearts (breakable)
Love (enough for two)
1/2 cup of disappointment (frustration will also do)
Some hurt
3 cups of self-raising flour
Water
A pinch of patience to taste

COOKING INSTRUCTIONS

Preheat your oven at 450 degrees.

Take two people and fold them together using your hands. They will be tough to start with but will eventually loosen when combined with attraction, so add liberally. When both people are completely intertwined, roll into a ball and cover with a damp cloth.

Next, put the bravado into a large mixing bowl and add the insecurities. Before long, the bravado will begin to disappear, leaving you with a bowl full of insecurities. Set aside to cool. In another bowl, add half of the intimacy, half of the secrets, the eggs and all of the expectations. Mix well.

Now for the tricky part. Slowly add time and familiarity. Careful it doesn't spoil. Keep stirring. If it starts to burn, just add any leftover patience you have. Dip your finger in and taste—if it is sweet, stop stirring and let it sit. If it is sour, throw away and start again using fresh ingredients. Simply wait for the right person to come into season before beginning again.

Break the hearts into a large pot. Set over a high heat while slowly adding disappointment and hurt. Stir constantly while the disappointment and hurt simmer down to a steam, then remove the hearts. (Watch out, they're hot!)

Place the hearts into the bowl of eggs and expectations, and add the rest of your secrets and intimacy. Leave in fridge to set.

Check on the insecurities. By now, they should have completely evaporated, but if not, just keep adding time until there is nothing left.

When the hearts are set (their breaks will be repaired and will be hard to the touch), place in a deep baking dish with flour and water. Pierce skins of hearts with a fork. Then pour in the love. Be generous. They will soak it up.

Now place the baking dish in the oven and let bake until the cake is perfect.

Which will be never.

So relax.

GOLD

It's a pitiful fool who will hopelessly drool
And obsess for a valuable gemstone or jewel,
But a fool I became in my desperate demise
When I first met the girl with the gold in her eyes.

Oh, how I was thrilled by that breathtaking gild,
A brilliant and blinding goldmine to be drilled
So, a devious plan I began to devise—
A plan to abscond with the gold in her eyes.

As I woke, as I slept, its siren song kept
Captivating and baiting my thoughts till I wept,
And a madness took hold as I ached for the prize
That lay buried within those incredible eyes.

T'was a madness indeed, for the want became need
And the need turned to hunger, the hunger to greed,
And filled with the heat of a thousand Julys
I longed to be rich with the gold in her eyes.

In visions I saw a spectacular aura
Surrounding the gold like an emerald aurora.
Oh yes, like the glow in the northernmost skies,
So too I saw jade in those treasure chest eyes.

What delusions were these? Surely this was a tease,
Just tricks of the mind or some cruel fantasies.
But it soon became clear this was no dark disguise,
There really were jewels buried deep in her eyes.

And I swear that it's true, there was tanzanite too,
If you looked past the gold and the green there was blue!
And surrounding those opaline stones of surprise
There were millions of pearls in the whites of her eyes.

It didn't stop there, I found riches most rare
In the splinters of amber that marbled her hair.
On her nose and her cheeks wherein each freckle lies,
Red diamonds to add to the gold in her eyes.

When the angle is right, look close and you might

29

See the rubies adorning her lips in the light.
Lo, my cup overflows with the wealth she supplies—
I am rich from much more than just gold in her eyes.

I pause now that I have this trove and I try
To list all the extravagant things I could buy.
But my list fades to naught just as I realize
I'd know not what to do with the gold in her eyes.

See the truth must be told that I've no need for gold
Or metals or minerals that ought to be sold.
I'm scornful of that which a wealthy man buys
If I can't have the girl with the gold in her eyes.

While jewels she has many, I do not need any,
I'm rich without even a solit'ry penny.
I'm already blessed with the ultimate prize
See, the treasure's the girl, not the gold in her eyes.

She makes kings appear broke; turns their lucre to smoke
For without her the thought of their fortune's a joke.
I pity them all now that I have grown wise
And see such abundance as cavernous lies.
For there's no richer man under all of God's skies
Than the boy with the girl with the gold in her eyes.

SAND
–for Alexandra

When you swim from the ocean and come to the land
And crawl on the beach and bury each hand,
Then you look at them both when you rise up to stand,
You see sure enough they are covered with sand.

Of the trillions and trillions of grains on the beach,
A tiny amount ended up in your reach.
And of all of the sand that you touched, it is true
Even less, you discover, will stay stuck to you.

And life kind of works in much the same way—
Out of all of the people you meet every day,
Most of them come and they go pretty quick,
But only a few of the good ones will stick.

For after deserting the shore, back on land,
You find, stuck to you, the sparkle of sand.
And that, Alexandra, is one of your tricks
For you are the rare kind of person who sticks.

Of each and all people I've met, just my luck,
That I could meet you, and with me you've stuck.
Not the years nor the distance could ever erase
That beautiful person, that beautiful face.

When I bring all the memories we've shared to my mind,
There are just so few people as caring or kind
Or as funny or bright or thoughtful or grand—
Next to you, Alexandra, they're just grains of sand.

For over the years, all the people who met you,
The ones who you've touched will never forget you.
And if we were each but a grain in your hand
Just think of the castle you could build with that sand.

THE LIGHTHOUSE KEEPER

On a jagged cliff a lighthouse stood,
Its winking eye the sole care
Of the lighthouse keeper, who nightly would
Warn travelers as best he could,
And have them all dock safely there.

But this lighthouse was a different one.
Of others it was not alike,
For it powered not on spark or sun
But rather did this lighthouse run
On wheel turns of the keeper's bike.

He'd fixed it so it flanked his globe,
Attached in such a way that when
The light would dim it meant he'd slowed—
But sure enough, the beacon glowed
Much brighter when he sped again.

The keeper pedaled every night;
He'd never stop, he'd never doze,
He vigilantly kept his light
Turning true and burning bright,
Resting only when the sun arose.

And sailors all did understand
That though the keeper seldom slept
He always had them safely land.
They thought him steady and as faithful and
As brilliant as the light he kept.

But one night a hellish storm passed o'er
And turned the clear night sky dark grey.
It brought with it a huge downpour—
The sea grew wild, the wind did roar,
The storm clouds hid the moon away.

The lighthouse keeper ne'er had seen
A tempest full of more mischief.
The fog and wind and rain did seem
To swallow the lighthouse's beam
A yard or two beyond the cliff.

So, he rode his bike with increased speed,
The power in his body surged.
As the sweat dripped from him bead by bead
He swore that fateful night that he'd
Ride on until the sun emerged.

But the sun did not emerge at all.
Instead, it stayed eternal night.
For days on end the horrid squall
Had slowed the keeper to a crawl—
But on he rode, no end in sight.

The lighthouse keeper surely knew
As long as there were ships at sea
Precisely what he had to do
To keep his winking light in view.
So he struggled on relentlessly.

When the light began to lose its glow
The man wished that his legs were stronger.
And as the wheels turned soft and slow
He wept awhile, for he did know
He could not pedal for much longer.

His body shook, his joints were sore,
He'd spent himself there was no doubt.
Though he wanted to ride on for sure,
He could simply ride that bike no more—
And finally, the light went out.

Suddenly the storm abated
Faster than it did appear.
Rain and hailstones dissipated,
The absence of the wind created
Stillness in the night, now clear.

Then a star appeared where clouds had been,
And while the lighthouse keeper swore
It was more radiant and keen
Than any star he'd ever seen,
He had not seen it there before.

It shone so sharp and burned so bright
The keeper now could not help thinking
One did not need the lighthouse light,
For travelers would be alright
By following the star that's winking.

And now he has no need for bikes,
The keeper man who ne'ermore keeps.
Against the toil he raged those nights
The restful man no longer fights,
For finally he sleeps.

THE SPARROW

While I was walking through the park I met a sparrow.

"Hello, Sparrow," I said to the sparrow.

"Oh, I'm not a sparrow," said the sparrow. "I'm an eagle."

I was surprised, for I was certain he was a sparrow.

"You look like a sparrow," I said.

"That may be so," said the sparrow, "but I am in fact an eagle."

"But eagles are quite big," I said to the sparrow. "You are not big at all. On the contrary, you are quite small."

And into the face of logic the sparrow replied, "I am an eagle."

Thinking that perhaps I had been misinformed about the differences between sparrows and eagles, I pointed to another sparrow perched in a nearby tree and asked, "Is that then an eagle?"

"Don't be ridiculous," the sparrow laughed. "That's a sparrow."

I was very confused. "But you look just like that sparrow," I said. "How are you different?"

And the sparrow was quiet. When he finally spoke, his face had become sad and his voice soft. "I am an eagle," was all he said.

I looked at the sparrow for a long time and was filled with a great pity for him. "You must be very lonely," I said.

And the sparrow started crying. Just like an eagle.

MY SWEET TOOTH HEART

I recollect quite tenderly
The day my heart did call on me—
I let him in and sat him down
And asked him if he'd like some tea.
He said he did, and liked it brown,
And then I watched him quietly drown
Five sugars in it, while I sat
Across him in my dressing gown.

Then kicking off our little chat
I mentioned innocently that
I thought it odd we'd never met
Before this strange encounter at
The table by my kitchenette.
"You live inside my chest and yet
I've ne'er seen you before," said I
With timbre thickened by regret.

Before I got to ask him why
He chose today to stop on by,
My heart said, "Please forgive me though
The truth is that I'm rather shy."
I asked my heart wherefore and so
He lifted up his shirt to show
Me scratches, bite marks, every scar
Of fierce frays fought long ago.

He said, "These gruesome markings are
The proof of all my fights thus far.
The awful heartbreaks that you've had
Become for me, a grim memoir.
As such, these defects make me sad."
To which I said, "I think they add
Some mystery and a just a tad
More character and attitude.
I really think they're not so bad."

This put him in a better mood
For then he said, "Each bitter feud
Has actually made me very strong.

I know that looking at me you'd
Not know that, and don't get me wrong
I do not want to make a song
And dance about the fact, but now
I'll prove it, if you'll play along."

Intrigued, I raised my puzzled brow
And asked my heart, quite simply, "How?"
He flexed his arm and motioned "Please..."
I did as I was told and—wow!
He barely budged within my squeeze,
His muscles hard like trunks of trees.
Indeed, this came as a surprise;
He did not look like Hercules.

I told my heart, "No one denies
You have more strength than you have size.
You're tougher than you seem to be."
And then he stared into my eyes
And whispered to me solemnly,
"All my force, my potency
Resides and ever grows in you,
Thus, you own all the strength in me."

Though what my heart had said was true,
His brawn to mine I could accrue,
I'd still a question yet to pray
And so, I asked him, "Why have you
Stopped over? I mean, why today?"
And then my heart did softly say,
"I've had of late a feeling which
Has filled me with a quiet dismay."

"I'm different, jumpy, like a switch
Has caused my ordered beats to glitch.
I'm swollen to the point I'll burst,
My panic's now at fever pitch."
I shook my head and smiled at first,
And watched him as he gravely cursed,
But worried not, for I knew why
He really needn't fear the worst.

I quelled his qualm with my reply,
"I should have told you, heart, but I
Have fallen quite in love, you see,
And that is why you feel awry."
"In love?" he cried out joyously,
"Well, that explains my frailty!"
He drew a flustered breath and then
Asked, "What's she like? Please, do tell me?"

"Well, if you took a perfect ten,
And squared that sum, not even then
Is it a fraction of the woman who
I now adore," I gushed, "And when
She walks into the room, it's true,
I quickly feel my heart, well, you—
Leap up into my throat and pump
Much faster than you norm'lly do."

"But what about the times I thump
Off key?" he asked. "Or when I jump
Around your chest in some frenzy?"
"That's her!" I said. "She need just bump
Past me to make you feel you're out at sea."
He scoffed. "And when I grow to be
Ten times my size?" I scoffed as well.
"That's surely when she's kissing me."

I carried on, "But though I fell
In love, I think it's fair I tell
You there may be some times you throb
In agony, but what the hell—
You're tough. You're strong. Let nothing rob
You of that fact, for should I sob
Or scream, grow scared, break down, I know
That you will do a brilliant job."

I asked him if he'd stay, but no
He couldn't, so I stood to show
My sweet tooth heart the door but knew
He'd take some macaroons to go.
Before he disappeared from view
He turned to me and said, "Thank you.

I like this one. I really do."
All I could say was, "Yeah. Me too."

MATCH

There are things in this world that are fine on their own,
They work perfectly when they're adrift and alone.

But most things do not, most things need adjunction,
They need a companion or else they won't function.

Like a flower without sunshine, or a car with no clutch,
Or a man with a limp trying to walk with no crutch.

And the frame of a racquet is useless, it's true,
With no strings in the middle, the balls travel through.

A cake with no flour, a tent with no pole,
They'd sink in the center and cease to be whole.

And water is made up of two things we know,
Without hydrogen, H2O is just O.

The words of old Egypt would never be known
Were it not for the help of one ancient stone.

And speaking of stones, every arch would go tumbling
Without keystones present to keep them from crumbling.

A camera needs some sort of storage inside it
As well as a flash or the darkness will hide it.

There are so many things that work better in twos,
Like bacon and eggs, or chopsticks, or shoes.

And I am no different, I'm simply not done
As a solo, a single, an indie, a one.

Like having conditioner and lacking shampoo,
I am just incomplete if I haven't got you.

I am Europe connected to your Orient,
You're my half, you're my other, my 50%.

I'm a drum underneath your melodious flute,
I am falling t'wards earth and you're my parachute.

You're the air that inflates, I'm the lucky balloon,
Without you I'd shrink and I'd fly round the room.

I'm the itch, you're the scratch, I'm the lock, you're the latch,
I'm the wick of a candle and you are my match.

It's fractions, it's decimals, it's laws and quadratics,
We make absolute sense, like basic mathematics.

So what do you say, my times two, my squared —
Sorrow is halved and joy's doubled when shared.

Come take my hand and adventure will find us,
Our shadows grow long as the sun sets behind us.

When the moon displaces her partner, the sun,
Split the space that's between us so that two become one.

THE TINY LADY

There once was a lady,
Her stature so small
She stood up to maybe
Just two inches tall.

But if you got near
Then doubtless you'd see
Her allure become clear—
A boundless beauty.

Her eyes like fruit brandy,
Her skin, peanut butter,
Her nose like a candy,
Her lips like no other.

Her hair falling heavy
Like ropes of licorice,
Her whole face a heady
And heavenly dish.

My mouth began drooling,
My stomach was rumbling,
My hunger was grueling,
My patience was crumbling.

Each part satisfying
My mouth-wetting wishes,
There was no denying
She's just too delicious!

My grin grew to greedy,
She was mine to sup.
When no one could see me
I snatched her right up.

From my fingers she clung
Like a sweet jelly baby,
Then on to my tongue,
And I swallowed the lady.

And then what I tasted

Defies definition,
My words will be wasted
But with your permission…

She tasted like fire,
She tasted like ice,
I tasted desire,
And then paradise.

She tasted like yearning
But also like calm,
My tongue was still burning
When I felt a qualm.

The lady was wriggling
Inside of my throat,
And then I heard giggling
As if she did gloat.

Before I distended
She swam like a mullet
And soon she'd descended
The length of my gullet.

The next thing I knew
She was inside my lungs
Where she bounced fro and to
And played them like drums.

She found my blood line
And surfed through my veins,
She scaled up my spine
And burrowed my brains.

Then she did dart
To my chest and just sorta
Slipped into my heart
Right through the aorta

She set up a bed
'Neath the atrial dome,
This pump turned instead
From my heart to her home.

And there she's resided
'Til this very day,
It's clear she's decided
That she's there to stay

I thought I had doomed her
When I gulped her down.
I thought I'd consumed her—
It was the other way round.

BETTER

You say you've found love, that you fit like a glove
With a person right down to the letter.
You deserve this fine fate, for your person sounds great,
But just FYI, mine is better.

You say you're a pair; she's the fuel, you're the air
In the engine of love's carburetor.
I take nothing away, I hope, when I say
That mine still sounds just a bit better.

Sure, it's not a contest to see who's the best
Every man is himself his bar-setter
But if we *were* keeping score, and we're not, but for sure
If we were you would see that mine's better.

Look, I'm sure yours is fine—I mean not next to mine—
But I'm sure she'd impress if I met 'er
For you say she is witty and clever and pretty
Okay, blah blah blah, mine's still better.

Of my competitive streak I have heard people speak,
But that's gone now, I promise I'm better.
For a love that is shared can't be matched or compared
But a person *can* be, and mine's better.

If you think that I prate, 'cause you've found your soulmate
Whose love warms your heart like a sweater,
Then let deafness befall comparisons all—
All but mine, because clearly mine's better.

And though you persist that I'm wrong and insist
That my love chokes my sense like a fetter,
It's simply not true, for you get a prize too
And silver's still good, but gold's better.

So while I take the cup, and you take runner-up,
There's no shame to be bested by better.
Put my love against any person dispensed,
Including myself, she's still better.

I can't, I concur, hold a candle to her,

I'm a toy gun while she's a Beretta
Which is why, I believe, she may very well leave
When she figures out she can do better.

And so, I, every day, to get her to stay
Try to be just a little bit better.
I know *not* if that will make her stick 'round, but still
For the sake of my poor heart, she'd better.

And to all, I am callin', who've found one and fallen
With faith like the fix of a setter,
Then you know, as I do, what is doubtlessly true,
That love makes life just a bit better.

So, with all that in mind, if you're lucky to find
Your other, then heed my behest—
In life's operetta, no "one love" is better...
Except mine, because mine's the best.

EMILY

Emily, oh Emily, that name is so heavenly
But it's so hard to rhyme with when you say it phonetically.
The unfortunate verity when dealing with Emily
Is apparently "Emily" is sort of a rarity,
Having plenty of energy but no consonant parity.
So poetically Emily contains no more symmetry
Than a cheap dime store effigy or a faded facsimile
Or a once great celebrity now altered synthetically.
But the remedy may be an Emily simile—
Like Emily's Emily, the way lemons are lemony.
Apologies, Emily, for that simile felony,
You're probably cleverly quietly condemning me
For what is effectively poetic obscenity.
But spare me the penalty and show me some charity
For there's no greater punishment mentally than for me
To feel Emily's enmity or be Emily's enemy.
For incredibly Emily to me is like family
So that every sensory memory of Emily
Has essentially always been us versus them and we
Found unexpectedly we have this rare chemistry,
An alchemy found in a recipe probably.
For verily Emily merrily mirrors me,
And hopefully Emily mercifully marries me,
So that Emily and I can be like ebony and ivory.
Which brings me to my summary, and pardon my prolixity,
But basically it's destiny that I ally with Emily
In perfect unanimity, for if you take her melody
And pair it with my cadency, you'll find with utmost certainty
The only rhyme for Emily there'll ever really be is me.
The harmony's off key, you see, til "he" and "she" turn into "we."
For that is perfect poetry: me and my sweet Emily.

DICTIONARY

The millions of words in our vocabulary
Have each been assigned definition, and hence
There is limited meaning a word represents.
But when talking to you there is no dictionary
That pinpoints my purpose or sums up my sense.

See for you, I've a language you don't understand,
A recondite tongue that is spoken not read
So there's no lexicon to define it, instead
Let this be your guide to my lingual short hand
Where what's meant is so rarely akin to what's said.

When I say "Hello" I do not mean "Hi,"
I mean, "You are the most precious thing to me, so
While my aim is to make your life great, you should know
I can't promise I will, but I promise I'll try."
See, that's what I mean if I'm saying "Hello."

And when I say "Goodnight" you may be unaware
That I really mean "Please still be here when I rise.
Will you please be the vision that first meets my eyes?
For if not, I'll stay sleeping and dream that you're there."
Yes, that is what uttering "Goodnight" implies.

If I'm trying to tell you "Beyond any doubt,
You are dazzling in every conceivable way,
That your beauty is rich as if drawn by Monet
That to me you are perfect"—that will not come out.
"You look lovely" will likely be all that I say.

And "How are you?" translates to "I still can't believe
How lucky—in spite of my failings and through
All the clutter in life—I stumbled on you."
"I miss you" just means "If you were to leave
I honestly don't know just what I would do."

"Hey there" is how I evasively say
"I'll be yours, without question, I promise you this."
While "Hey" on its own means "Let's reminisce
On our story as lovers when we're old and grey,
When all that I'll want or I'll need is your kiss."

"Yes" means "I'm longing to vanish within
The infinite sea of your perfect embrace."
While "No" means "I may disagree with your case,
But I'm yours for the bidding when I touch your skin
Or fall for the figure and form of your face."

If you hear my voice rise in an impassioned spar,
It's masking my truthful but unspoken cry
Of "Darling, I'm scared that soon you'll see I
Am not nearly enough for the woman you are."
There'll be times when that happens, but now you'll know why.

There may even be times, for my language is young,
When words, whims and whispers I cannot define,
Escape with the likely assistance of wine—
If and when that occurs, you must silence my tongue
By instantly pressing your lips against mine.

I know it's unclear, this complex glossary,
But it's not *all* behind a semantic smoke screen.
I've one phrase allusion does not contravene,
A single entendre, without irony—
When I tell you "I love you," that is just what I mean.

THE SEAFARING MAN

A seafaring man went sailing one day,
His intention to travel quite far, far away
Though where he was going, he just couldn't say
He simply did cherish the sea.

It'd been a long time for he'd had a close call
When he wrecked his last boat in a horrible squall
And it took his heart years to summon the gall
To again brave the water, you see.

As he looked on the beach when he pulled from the shore
He realized a thought he'd not realized before:
Whatever adventures the sea had in store,
He'd ne'er again look on this sand.

With a mist in his eye, he then had the notion
To raise the main sail, and the sheet sprang to motion.
The man and his boat once again skimmed the ocean,
The fire within him re-fanned.

The hours became days, and the days became weeks,
The sun warmed his face and reddened his cheeks,
The water was calm and the boat sprang no leaks,
His journey could not have been better.

But then without warning the wind picked up pace,
So he tied every rope and he screwed every brace
And he plucked up his courage from a fathomless place
As the air became darker and wetter.

The sea tossed the boat and 'twas useless to steer
And the seafaring man was filled with a fear
That surely the end of his life had drawn near
And he prayed for the tempest to cease.

As if hearing his prayer, the weather did ease,
The wind settled down to a temperate breeze,
The spray from the waves no more strength than a sneeze
And the sea once again found her peace.

A queer thing then happened in the wake of the gale—

The wind in the air simply stopped and grew stale
And as hard as he tried the boat just wouldn't sail.
He found himself now in a jam.

For he knew that unless there was some change of weather
He may well be stuck out in this boat forever
And in what the man knew was a desperate endeavor,
He leapt from his boat and he swam.

He could see in the distance some small form of land,
So he paddled his feet and threw hand over hand
And continued this stroke until he hit sand
Then he rested a moment on shore.

It was right in that instant the wind gathered speed
And he suddenly rued his hasty misdeed
For he watched as the size of his boat did recede
Until he could see it no more.

The seafaring man sat alone on the isle
And wasted the days for what seem like a while
Though the trees bore sweet fruit and the ground was fertile,
He longed to be back on the brine.

So, he cut down some trees and tore strips from his coat—
With this crude equipment he fashioned a boat
And when he was certain the vessel would float
He left the sandy shoreline.

While the new boat was smaller than the last one, indeed
What it lacked in its size it made up for in speed,
And besides it had all that a sailor could need,
And this one could not disagree.

Now the seafaring man sails for day upon day
In a boat that he found in a curious way,
Though where he is going, he just cannot say,
He simply does cherish the sea.

THE MAGIC WORD

Pick a card, any card—
No wait, this trick is not that hard.
I'll roll my sleeves up one and two
And magic I will do for you.

Look inside this hat and there
You'll find my little friend the hare.
You're not impressed? Just wait there's more!
I'll dazzle you with feats of awe.

A blade this sharp, you may well wonder
How I saw this girl asunder.
I'll juggle clubs, I'll spin this plate
I'll close my eyes and levitate.

No please come back, you can't abscond
There's magic in this little wand.
I'll read your mind, this mighty seer,
But it won't work without you here.

Lock me up and lose the key,
No handcuff can imprison me.
I'll hold my breath in icy drink—
What else to do? Just let me think.

But no, you will not watch the show
Where is it that you'd rather go?
No matter what goes in the mix
The problem is you know my tricks.

For when I show you up my sleeve
You turn your back and go to leave,
And lo this prestidigitator
Fears a cruel illusion later.

Yes, magic tricks I know galore—
The best ones that you ever saw.
But when you leave and vanish here
I cannot make you reappear.

I'll click my fingers, wave my stick

In vain to pull off one last trick.
If you had stayed you might have heard
Me whispering the magic word.

The curtain falls, the show is done,
The grand finale's yet to come.
The greatest magic there will be
Is having you come back to me.

THE BOOK THAT I READ LONG AGO

When I go to the back of my house, down the stairs,
I come to an old storage room, in which there's
An abundance of sad souvenirs that I stow
Where I find an old book that I read long ago.

When I see it I ask myself, *Why did I stash*
For so long a book that appears to be trash?
But when looking again I remember, oh no
There's more to this book that I read long ago.

Its pages are torn and its cover is cracked,
Both the proof of a care that clearly it lacked
And because of the years that it's spent down below,
There's now mold on this book that I read long ago.

The pages have been tattered over the years
And most of the corners are creased with dog-ears
And to read the front cover I carefully blow
All the dust from this book that I read long ago.

But look past the wear and the torn leather skin,
What makes this book special is what lies within.
While the print is now missing its once vibrant glow,
I can still read the book that I read long ago.

Its words are so simple and perfect that I'm
Reminded at once of a happier time.
Yes, emotions thought dormant are starting to flow
As I reread the book that I read long ago.

There are chapters in youth I did not understand
That now make absolute sense to me and
I realize I've now read too much to stop, so
I keep reading the book that I read long ago.

There are words I can't read for they're blurred with dark smears
Where I once must have wet the black ink with my tears
And again it would seem, I cannot fight the woe
For I cry o'er the book that I read long ago.

At the part I recalled was the end, I admit

The book did continue as if it were writ
Long after I dumped it down here where I throw
All my dusty old books that I read long ago.

As I read the new pages I am doubtlessly sure
That I've not ever read these additions before
But I'm learning new things, things that teach me to grow—
The teacher? A book that I read long ago.

And then when I finish, what seems like a prank,
Are pages and pages that look to be blank.
And I recollect instantly why I did stow
So finely this book that I read long ago.

The book is unique for it hasn't an end.
See, time is its author and life's how it's penned,
So each time I flip through the pages I know
There'll be more in the book that I read long ago.

I set the book back in its place on the floor,
I turn off the light, and I lock up the door,
And I'm sad as I realize I simply don't know
When I'll next read the book that I read long ago.

That extraordinary book I read long, long ago.

Made in the USA
Columbia, SC
23 May 2020